pearls from
Jo Seaga
kitchen

pearls from
Jo Seagar's
kitchen

PHOTOGRAPHY BY JOHN DALEY

RANDOM HOUSE
NEW ZEALAND

Published by

Random House New Zealand

18 Poland Road, Glenfield, Auckland, New Zealand

First published 1999

Designed by Christine Cathie

ISBN 1 86941 403 9

Printed by Spectrum Print, Christchurch

Contents

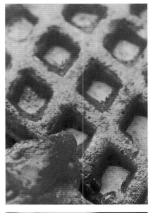

The main event

Vegetables, side dishes and dressings

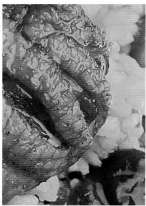

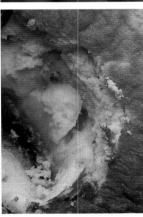

Breads and baking

Desserts

After-dinner treats

Dedicated to the loving memory of Antonia Reynolds

Acknowledgments

My sincere appreciation and thanks to Harriet Allan, my very patient and skilful publisher at Random House. And to Michael Moynahan, Managing Director of Random House, for his wise counsel and generous encouragement.

Special thanks to PA Annabelle Ullrich for all her help: testing, tasting, typing, and most of all for talking it all through and keeping me on schedule. I couldn't do what I do without you, Annabelle.

Thanks to my dear friend and fabulous photographer John Daley, who is so clever. And as always fondest love to Ross, Katie and Guy and my dear mother Fay, who help make it all happen and keep me smiling.

Introduction

The secret to a great dinner party is not the amount of time spent in the kitchen preparing, but in the amount of time enjoying one another's company. I've always maintained that just because a meal is incredibly complicated to cook and you've spent a fortune on food and used every item of kitchen paraphernalia you own, doesn't automatically mean it's going to be the most fabulously successful dinner party of all time.

It really is 'only dinner'. So don't panic. After all, what comes out of a guest's mouth in conversation is far more important than what food actually goes in. There's more to it than fuel. My philosophy is food for the easy life — shortcuts with style. Big flavours to suit modern tastes and easy-peasy recipes that really work.

We approach cooking with many shades of intensity, and I'm the first to admit that some of my cooking disasters have become a part of family legend. But, actually, mastering entertaining etiquette is not as gruelling as some would have you think. It's easier than a Samurai initiation ceremony, for example. And let's face it, friends do quickly tire of the non-reciprocating cook; so get out your pinny (even you blokes can be 'home on the range') and read on, because help is at hand.

I don't have the time or inclination to start preparing on Tuesday for Saturday dinner parties. I love entertaining but I don't want to spend all day in the kitchen, rather I want to establish memories with my dinner parties. So this book is about quick-fix meals, with ease of preparation, cups and spoons for measurements, flexibility of ingredients, no hard-to-pronounce let-alone hard-to-procure items (such as, olives from your hillside villa in Tuscany, kind of thing), and no flamboyant hard-to-master technique or terminology (I won't ask you to sweat those leeks, use chine, flambé or infuse). Keep it simple.

I see no point in bringing together textures and flavours that have absolutely nothing to offer one another. I've worked at this collection of recipes until I think they can be no better, but nothing's carved in stone. The variables are your own taste and, remember, it's entertaining; it's an occasion where you're allowed to liberate yourself. My policy is delicious trade-offs, such as healthy low-fat vegetable nibbles for an indulgent dessert.

This book is all about enjoying good food, not giving it up when your cooking repertoire gradually diminishes. You no longer have to end up constantly preparing menus 1, 2 or 3 of tried and true recipes that readily come to mind. My hope is that this new collection will increase your scope and range.

So put on your pearls and get cooking!

Brunch

Lemon poppy-seed muffins with fresh lemon syrup or lemon cream-cheese frosting

Makes 12

2 eggs, lightly beaten

1 cup sour cream

½ cup milk

¼ cup oil

3 tablespoons honey

¼ cup poppy seeds

grated rind of 1 lemon

2¼ cups self-raising flour

Lemon syrup

juice of 2 lemons

3 tablespoons caster sugar

Lemon cream-cheese frosting

½ cup approx cream-cheese, softened

¾ cup icing sugar

1 tablespoon lemon juice

1 teaspoon grated lemon rind

Place eggs, sour cream, milk, oil, honey, poppy seeds, lemon rind and flour in a bowl. Mix until just combined. Spoon mixture into deep, greased muffin tins. Bake for 15–20 minutes at 180°C until cooked and golden. The muffins can be eaten plain or topped with syrup or frosting. For the syrup mix the ingredients together then pour over while the muffins are still warm. Cool on a wire rack. To prepare the frosting, place cream cheese, icing sugar, lemon juice and rind in a food processor. Process until smooth. Top cold muffins with icing.

Lemon poppy-seed muffins with lemon cream-cheese frosting Inset: with fresh lemon syrup

Banana wheatgerm muffins
Makes 12

1½ cups flour

¾ cup sugar

1 tablespoon baking powder

½ teaspoon salt

¾ cup wheatgerm

1½ cups mashed ripe bananas (approx 3)

½ cup milk

2 eggs

¼ cup vegetable oil

1 teaspoon vanilla extract

Pre-heat oven to 200°C. In a large bowl mix together all the ingredients until just combined. Spoon mixture into standard-size greased muffin tins. Bake for 20–25 minutes. Remove muffins from tin and cool on a wire rack.

*Banana wheatgerm
muffins*

Oat-meal pancakes
Makes 16 pancakes

4 eggs

2 cups milk (approx)

2 cups self-raising flour

1 cup oat-meal

½ cup brown sugar

In a food processor or bowl mix everything together to a smooth spoonable batter. Add a little extra milk if too thick. Grease a non-stick frypan and drop tablespoons of the mixture into the pre-heated pan and cook over medium heat until golden brown, 2–3 minutes. Turn over and cook other side. Stack pancakes on a plate and cover with a teatowel to keep pancakes warm and soft. Serve with maple syrup, whipped cream or yoghurt and fresh fruit.

Individual eggs benedict soufflés
Serves 6

6 eggs

½ cup cream

1 cup ham, finely chopped

1 cup cheese, grated

salt and freshly ground black pepper

6 muffins, split in half and toasted

1 tablespoon parsley, chopped to garnish

Blender lemon hollandaise

4 egg yolks

juice and grated zest of 1 lemon

1 tablespoon white-wine vinegar

salt and freshly ground black pepper

200 g hot melted butter plus 100 g extremely soft barely melted
   butter (as though it's been sitting on the bench in the hot sun)

Pre-heat oven to 150°C. Choose ³/₄-cup sized ramekins or individual soufflé moulds and generously grease and line their bases with a circle of baking paper. Whisk together eggs and cream. Mix in ham, cheese and salt and freshly ground black pepper. Divide mixture between the cups. Place these in a roasting pan and add enough water to come halfway up the sides of the ramekins. Bake for approximately 1 hour until the soufflés remain firm in the centre when gently shaken.

To make blender hollandaise, place yolks in a blender or food processor and mix. Through the feed tube with the machine running slowly add the lemon juice, zest, white-wine vinegar and salt and pepper. The yolks should be light, pale and creamy. Slowly drizzle in the hot melted butter then mix in the barely melted softened butter. Taste and add extra salt and pepper as needed.

Remove soufflés from water. Run a small sharp knife around the sides to loosen. Unmould each soufflé onto the toasted muffins. Peel off the paper and pour over hollandaise sauce and garnish with chopped parsley.

*Individual eggs
benedict soufflés*

delicious breakfast dish similar to classic eggs benedict but
nout all the fiddle. The eggs remain soft and creamy. This mixture
also be made in one large dish and sliced or spooned out onto

How to poach eggs

Fill a wide deep pan halfway with water. Bring the liquid to a rolling boil over high heat, then reduce the heat so that the liquid barely simmers. Break and drop in as many eggs as needed. Or break the eggs, one at a time, into a saucer and slide them into the pan. As each egg is dropped in, push the egg white back immediately towards the yolk with a large slotted spoon, moving the egg gently. Simmer the eggs for $2\frac{1}{2}$ minutes, transfer them with the slotted spoon to a pan of cold water, and let them stand until they are needed (a cunning tip used in restaurants). Trim the egg whites with scissors. If poached correctly the yolk will be covered completely by the white and the egg will have returned approximately to its original oval shape. To serve the eggs hot, reheat them in a saucepan of simmering water for 30 seconds, or until they are heated through.

Traditional eggs benedict

Serve poached eggs on toasted English muffins with a couple of slices of ham. Top with hollandaise sauce.

*Traditional eggs
benedict*

Waffles

Makes 8

3 eggs, separated

1½ cups milk

100 g butter, melted

2 tablespoons caster sugar

2 cups self-raising flour

1 teaspoon vanilla

oil spray or extra butter for greasing waffle iron

In a food processor or large bowl mix egg yolks, milk, melted butter, sugar, flour and vanilla. Mix to a smooth batter. In a separate bowl beat egg whites until stiff peaks form, then fold carefully into the batter.

Oil spray or brush a heated waffle iron with melted butter, spoon in 2–3 tablespoons of batter and cook until the waffles are crisp and golden brown. Serve warm with whipped cream, maple syrup, fresh fruit and crispy bacon.

Bacon tips

To cook really crispy bacon lay out rashers on a baking tray that has only a slight edge (or in a shallow roasting dish). Bake in a hot oven 200°C for about 10 minutes until crispy. Turn over and cook a further 5 minutes until the desired level of crispiness is achieved. Drain on paper towels and serve.

Orange cinnamon French toast

½ cup milk

½ cup caster sugar

3 eggs

1 teaspoon vanilla

½ teaspoon cinnamon

grated rind of 1 orange

6–8 thick slices French bread (day old bread is best), diagonally cut

butter or oil to fry in

icing sugar to dust

In a food processor or blender, mix milk, caster sugar, eggs, vanilla, cinnamon and orange rind. Pour into a shallow lasagne-type dish, then dip in the slices of bread. Heat butter or oil in a large frypan and fry both sides of bread until golden crispy brown. Dust with icing sugar and serve with sliced bananas or peaches, whipped cream and maple syrup.

Nibbles

Little French onion tarts

Makes 48

4 sheets frozen savoury pastry (Ernest Adams)

50 g butter

1 tablespoon olive oil

4 medium red onions, finely chopped

3 eggs

150 ml cream

salt and freshly ground black pepper

Cut circles of thawed pastry with a 5–6 cm cutter and press into mini muffin tins. Melt the butter and oil in a frypan and add chopped onion. Stir over a medium heat until softened and just lightly coloured, then remove from heat. In a bowl beat eggs and cream together. Add salt and freshly ground black pepper to taste and stir in the cooked onions. Pour mixture into pastry-lined cases and bake at 180°C for 20–25 minutes until the filling is set and the pastry is golden and crisp. Serve warm.

Little French
onion tarts

Dips

Serve in bowls surrounded by fresh vegetables or pita crisps.

Sweet chilli yoghurt dip

Makes 2 cups

500 g thick creamy natural yoghurt

3 cloves garlic, crushed (1 teaspoon)

½ cup parsley, chopped

½ cup coriander, chopped

1 tablespoon sweet chilli sauce

1 cup cucumber, finely chopped (optional)

or 3 spring onions, finely chopped (optional)

Mix together and keep in the fridge, covered, until required.

Green gherkin relish dip

Makes 2 cups

500 g thick creamy natural yoghurt or sour cream

130 g (½ jar) green gherkin relish

½ cup parsley, chopped

Mix together and keep in the fridge, covered, until required.

Ploughman's pickle dip

Makes 2 cups

500 g (approx 3 cups) sour cream

1 cup ploughman's pickle

2 tablespoon parsley, chopped

Mix together and keep in the fridge, covered, until required.

Yoghurt dip with
fresh vegetables
and pita crisps

Vegetables

Serve dips with a platter of fresh vegetables: celery, peppers, cucumber sticks, broccoli, cauliflower, carrot sticks, baby button mushrooms and courgettes. The firmer ones like carrots, cauliflower and broccoli should be blanched in boiling water for a minute or two then refreshed in cold water to keep them crisp and colourful.

Pita crisps

mini or small size pita breads

olive oil spray

garlic salt

Split the mini pita breads in half and cut into wedges with kitchen scissors. Generously spray a baking tray with olive oil, and on it place a single layer of pita wedges. Spray the wedges with olive oil and sprinkle with garlic salt. Bake at 180°C for 10–15 minutes, until crisp and golden. Cool on a wire rack and store in an airtight container.

Marinating olives

Drain jars or cans of olives in brine. Place in a clean jar or container and cover with good flavoured olive oil. Add flavours of your choice: fresh herb sprigs (rosemary, thyme, etc), finely peeled orange and lemon rind, chillies or dried chilli flakes, peppercorns, garlic, cumin, coriander seeds, etc. Store for at least 3 days to allow flavours to develop. Olives will keep for months this way as long as there is a good layer of oil over the top. Don't allow any olives to be exposed half out of the oil to the air.

Marinating feta cheese with olives

Add cubes of firm feta cheese to the olives but for safety store this in the fridge. The oil can look solid and cloudy when cold but will clear as it warms up to room temperature. Allow at least 3 days for flavours to start developing. Will keep for 3–4 weeks in the fridge.

Crostinis and vogelinis

To make crostinis, oil spray and bake 1 cm slices of French bread until crispy and golden. Or alternatively make vogelinis by trimming the crusts off thin slices of Vogels wholegrain bread, oil spray and bake until crisp and dry.

Spread with soft cream cheese and top with a little slice of smoked salmon giving it a small twist and swirl. Try to get height in the presentation. Garnish with a sprig of parsley, a thin strip of lemon peel or a tiny dollop of caviar (lumpfish roe). Plain fresh brown bread is also great topped with cream cheese, with smoked salmon and freshly ground black pepper.

Smoked salmon spread

250 g spreadable cream cheese

100 g (approx) or 1 cup loosely packed smoked salmon pieces
(offcuts or chopped slices)

3 tablespoons parsley, finely chopped

1 teaspoon of lemon pepper seasoning

optional: finely chopped chives, spring onion, capers, hardboiled egg
or fresh lemon juice

Mix until combined and smooth. Spread on crackers, toast or crostinis or use to fill mini cheese muffins.

Crostinis and vogelinis
with smoked salmon
and olives

Bacon and waterchestnuts

8 rashers streaky rindless bacon

250 g can waterchestnuts

garlic salt

bamboo skewers

Divide each rasher of bacon into four shorter strips. Wrap waterchestnuts in bacon. Thread in a line on skewers, leaving a small gap between each, sprinkle with garlic salt. Bake in a hot oven, 200°C, for about 15 minutes until crispy. Turn once to cook evenly. Serve by re-threading onto fresh individual bamboo skewers.

Mini toasted cheese muffins

Makes 36

2 cups flour	1 egg
4 teaspoons baking powder	¼ cup oil
½ teaspoon salt	1¼ cups milk
1 cup grated tasty cheese	

Stir all ingredients together in a large bowl, just lightly mixing to combine. Don't overwork the mixture or the muffins will be tough and heavy. Spoon the mixture, which should be fairly runny, into greased deep mini-muffin tins. Sprinkle with a few extra shreds of grated cheese. Bake in a hot oven 200°C for 15–20 minutes until golden brown.

Variations

To make savoury muffins, add any of the following to the toasted cheese muffin recipe: chopped herbs, finely sliced spring onions, nuts, a tablespoon of fruit chutney or relish, chopped pickled onions or gherkins, crumbled blue cheese, chopped ginger or crushed garlic.

Fill with dips, flavoured cream cheese, sliced brie and pickle or sour cream with smoked salmon.

Mini toasted cheese muffins filled with sour cream, smoked salmon and caviar

Oysters
Oyster shots with wasabi dressing

1 tablespoon wasabi paste or to taste

½ cup extra virgin olive oil

2 tablespoons white-wine vinegar

1 teaspoon sugar

salt and freshly ground black pepper

1 tablespoon parsley, finely chopped

1 oyster per person

In a small bowl mix with a wire whisk or place all ingredients but the oysters into a screw-top jar and shake vigorously until well blended and season with salt and freshly ground black pepper. Serve whole oysters in shot glasses with a splash of wasabi dressing.

Half-shell oysters

Serve oysters on a half shell with a little spoon of sour cream and some caviar, plus a tiny sprig of dill or parsley and squeeze of lemon.

LEFT: *Half-shell oysters*
RIGHT: *Oyster shots*

Simple cheese straws

Makes 40

2 sheets of thawed pre-rolled frozen puff or flaky pastry

1 cup grated tasty cheese (keep a bag of grated cheese in the freezer
   — it never goes mouldy and can be used from frozen)

garlic salt

Pre-heat oven to 200°C. Cut the pastry into strips approx 1 cm wide × 10 cm long (like a large French fry). Place on a tray lined with baking paper or a well-greased baking tray. Place the straws close together but not quite touching and sprinkle with grated cheese and dust with garlic salt. Bake for 8–10 minutes until puffed up, golden and crispy looking. Cool on a wire rack and store in an airtight container. These are nicest served warm: reheat in a low oven to heat and crisp up. For a 'hotted up' version give them a further sprinkle with a little chilli powder or cayenne pepper.

*Simple cheese
straws*

Filo cups filled with curried chicken and pineapple

Makes 24

16 sheets filo pastry

olive oil spray

Filling

1 cup thick prepared mayonnaise

1 teaspoon curry powder or curry paste to taste

½ cup crushed pineapple, drained

1 cup shredded cooked chicken or smoked chicken

1 tablespoon parsley, chopped

sprig parsley to garnish

In a bowl mix together all filling ingredients. Working quickly, remove 4 sheets of filo from the package. Spray filo sheets with oil to prevent them from drying out and cracking. Stack up 4 layers of filo pastry then cut into 6 squares with scissors. Spray 2 mini-muffin tins with oil spray. Press in a layered square of filo, carefully pushing down with your fingertips to form a little cup shape. Bake at 200°C for 5–6 minutes until golden brown. Cool on a wire rack. When cold place a spoonful of the chicken mixture in each filo pastry cup, garnishing with a sprig of parsley.

Filo cups filled with curried chicken and pineapple

Parmesan wafer biscuits

Makes 12 approx

> 1 cup grated parmesan cheese
> optional: ground cumin, caraway seeds, celery salt or sesame seeds
>   or freshly ground black pepper

Pre-heat oven to 200°C. Place small piles of grated parmesan cheese onto a tray lined with baking paper. Sprinkle with any optional extras. Bake for 5–6 minutes until crispy and golden.

Parmesan wafer biscuits

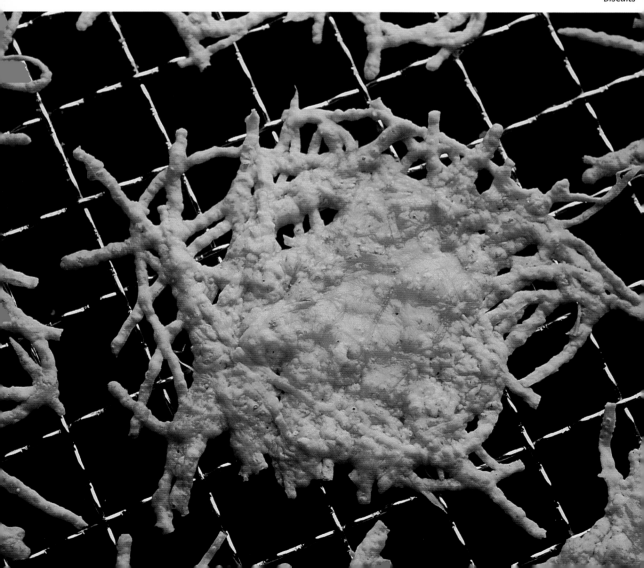

Soups and small courses

Fresh Italian soup
Serves 6

1 tablespoon olive oil

1 red onion, finely chopped

2–3 cloves garlic, crushed (1 teaspoon)

2 sticks celery, finely sliced

2 large tomatoes, chopped

½ telegraph cucumber, chopped

3 cups tomato juice

2 cans whole peeled tomatoes with their juice, chopped

1 teaspoon Worcester sauce

salt and lots of freshly ground black pepper

½ cup chopped fresh herbs (parsley, basil and chives)

Heat oil in a large saucepan. Add onion and garlic and stir-fry for 2 minutes to soften. Add all other ingredients, season to taste with salt and pepper and serve as soon as it heats up. No need to simmer this soup, it's best just quickly brought to the boil and eaten while the vegetables are still crisp.

Beer soup with stilton cheese

Serves 4

100 g butter

1 tablespoon olive oil

4–6 large onions, thinly sliced

4 cups beef stock

4 cups dark beer

salt and lots of freshly ground black pepper

1 French breadstick, cut into 1 cm slices (makes approx 10 slices)

olive oil spray

200 g/1 cup crumbled stilton cheese

2 tablespoons parsley, chopped

Heat butter and oil in a large frypan. Add onion and fry until brown and caramelised. Pour in the stock and beer, season with salt and pepper and simmer for 5 minutes. Spray slices of French bread with olive oil and toast both sides under a grill until golden. Place 2–3 slices of bread in each soup bowl or ramekin. Pour hot soup on top, then sprinkle with crumbled stilton. Place under grill until cheese bubbles and starts to brown (about 2 minutes). Sprinkle with chopped parsley and serve immediately.

Beer soup with
stilton cheese

French onion soup

Serves 4

100 g butter

1 tablespoon olive oil

4 onions, thinly sliced

8 cups beef stock

salt and lots of freshly ground black pepper

1 French breadstick, cut into 1 cm slices (makes approx 10 slices)

olive oil spray

½ cup grated gruyére cheese

2 tablespoons parsley, chopped

Heat butter and oil in a large frypan. Add onion and fry until brown and caramelised. Pour in the stock and season with salt and pepper and simmer for 45–50 minutes. Spray slices of French bread with olive oil and toast both sides under a grill until golden. Pour soup into a soup bowl or large ramekin, place a slice of bread on top sprinkled with gruyére cheese and place under grill until cheese bubbles and starts to brown (about 2 minutes). Sprinkle with chopped parsley and serve immediately.

Smoked seafood chowder
Serves 6

100 g butter

1 leek, finely sliced

1 medium onion, chopped

1 tablespoon flour

1 cup fish stock (use the liquid from the canned smoked fish)

2 cups milk

1 cup sweetcorn (fresh off the cob, frozen, canned or creamed)

1 potato, peeled and diced into small pieces

1 x 310 g can of smoked fish fillets, or 2 cups flaked smoked fish

2 cups (approx) mixed seafood

½ cup cream

½ cup parsley, chopped

salt and freshly ground black pepper

Heat the butter in a large saucepan add the sliced leek and onion. Stir-fry 3–4 minutes, then add the flour and stir well. Stir over a gentle heat and add the fish stock and milk. Add the corn, diced potato, smoked fish and other seafood. Gently simmer until potato is softened and the soup is smooth and thick. Finally add the cream and parsley and season to taste with pepper and a little salt (note that smoked fish tends to be quite salty).

Smoked seafood chowder

Pumpkin cinnamon soup
Serves 6

1 medium-sized pumpkin, peeled and roughly diced

1 large onion, chopped

2 cloves garlic, crushed (1 teaspoon)

200 g butter

1 teaspoon cinnamon (options: pinenuts, sweet chilli sauce, thyme,
   coriander)

a little milk

1¼ cups cream

salt and freshly ground black pepper

chopped parsley and yoghurt or cream to garnish

Just cover the pumpkin, onion and garlic with water and cook over a medium heat until the pumpkin is very soft and the water has mostly evaporated. Allow to cool slightly, then purée in a blender or food processor in batches, adding the butter and cinnamon with a little milk to thin the mixture if required. Return to the saucepan and stir in the cream and season with salt and pepper. Reheat gently, and serve garnished with chopped parsley and a swirl of yoghurt or cream.

Thai chicken and lemongrass soup

Serves 4

1 tablespoon oil

1 large onion, finely chopped

2–3 cloves garlic, crushed (1 teaspoon)

1 teaspoon ginger, crushed

1-2 tablespoons Thai green curry paste

1 x 400 ml can of coconut cream

1½ cups (approx 1 x 500 g carton) chicken stock

2 teaspoons lemongrass stems, crushed

1 double chicken breast, skinned, boned and sliced

½ cup fresh coriander, chopped

2 spring onions, finely sliced

salt and freshly ground black pepper

Heat oil in a large saucepan, add onion and cook 2–3 minutes until softened. Add garlic, ginger and curry paste and cook for a further minute, then stirring add coconut cream, chicken stock, chicken and lemongrass. Simmer covered for 10–15 minutes. Add coriander and spring onions and season with salt and pepper to taste.

Serve immediately.

Unbelievable smoked salmon and dill pie

Serves 4

Unbelievable because it's so easy to make and cooks like a self-crusting quiche: no need to fiddle about with a pastry layer first.

½ cup flour

5 eggs

1 tablespoon dill, finely chopped

60 g butter, softened

200 g smoked salmon pieces

1 onion, diced

salt and freshly ground black pepper

1 cup grated cheddar cheese

In a food processor place flour, eggs, dill and butter and process to combine. Pour egg mixture into a well-greased or oil-sprayed pie plate. Top with salmon, onion and salt and freshly ground black pepper to taste. Sprinkle with cheese. Bake at 180°C for 35–40 minutes or until mixture is set and top is golden brown.

Unbelievable smoked salmon and dill pie

Tuna spring-onion hot cakes with wasabi mayonnaise

Makes 6–8

1 x 425 g can chunky tuna packed in water

6 medium potatoes, peeled, cooked and mashed with a little butter

2 teaspoons curry powder (or curry paste, or sweet chilli sauce)

3 tablespoons parsley or coriander, chopped

2 eggs

2 spring onions, finely sliced

2 tablespoons flour

salt and freshly ground black pepper

flour to dust

In a bowl mix together all ingredients. Form into little patties with your fingers and dust with flour. Fry 2–3 minutes in hot oil. Turn and cook a further 1–2 minutes until golden all over. Serve with wasabi mayonnaise.

Wasabi mayonnaise

3 eggs yolks

2 teaspoons white-wine vinegar

1 tablespoon smooth Dijon mustard

½ teaspoon salt

200 ml olive oil

200 ml vegetable oil

2 tablespoons hot water

salt and freshly ground black pepper

1–2 teaspoons wasabi paste, to taste

2 tablespoons parsley

In food processor or blender mix egg yolks, white-wine vinegar, mustard and salt. With machine running, slowly drizzle in olive and vegetable oil. Whisk in 2 tablespoons hot water to stabilise mayonnaise. Season to taste and add 1–2 teaspoons wasabi paste and parsley.

Tuna spring-onion hot cakes with wasabi mayonnaise

Avocado with chilli prawn topping

Serves 6

3 firm ripe avocados

½ cup cooked small prawns

juice of 1 small lemon

1 tablespoon sweet chilli sauce

50 g butter

1 tablespoon flour

salt and freshly ground black pepper

1 cup milk

2 eggs, separated

1 cup tasty cheese, grated

fresh herbs, to garnish

Cut the avocados in half and remove stones. Make a small slice across the base of each half so they sit flat, cut side up. In a small bowl mix together prawns, lemon juice and sweet chilli sauce. Evenly divide the prawns between each half, filling the hollows left by the stones.

Melt butter in a small saucepan. Add the flour, salt and pepper. Gradually add the milk, whisking constantly until the sauce thickens. Whisk in the egg yolks and grated cheese. Stir until sauce is smooth and well combined. In a bowl beat the egg whites until stiff and carefully fold into the sauce. Place the avocados on a grill tray and spoon sauce over so that the top of each is completely covered. Place under a hot grill and cook until they are puffy and golden, about 3–4 minutes. Don't cook them for too long as the avocado flesh will turn bitter. Serve immediately, garnished with fresh herbs.

Avocado with chilli prawn topping

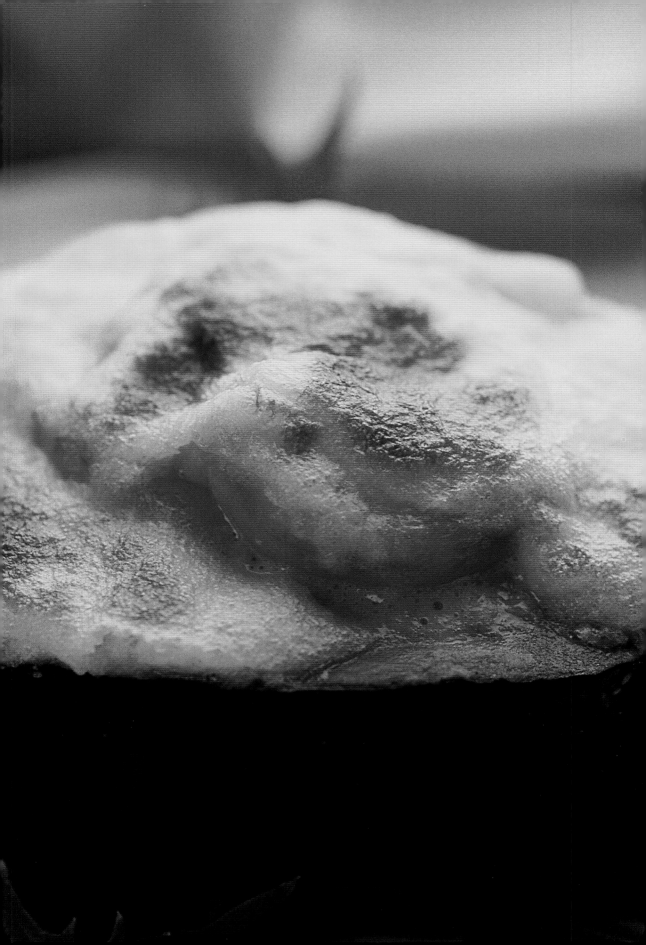

Strawberry, brie and avocado salad

Serves 4

1 cup (approx) strawberries, sliced

2 cups mixed salad leaves (mesclun, watercress, etc.)

1 firm but ripe avocado, sliced

250 g ripe brie cheese, cut into 8 slices

1 teaspoon coarsely ground pepper

Dressing

4 tablespoons olive oil

1 tablespoon balsamic vinegar

2 tablespoons fresh orange juice

grated rind ½ orange

Whisk together dressing ingredients. Toss together strawberries, salad leaves and avocado. Mix with the dressing and top with brie slices and pepper.

Fresh asparagus in puff pastry with lemon hollandaise

Serves 4–6

2 sheets pastry, thawed (frozen pre-rolled flaky or puff pastry)

1 egg yolk

1 tablespoon cold water

6–10 spears of asparagus per serving, depending on size of spears

Cut sheets of pastry into rectangles a little larger than a playing card. Spread out on a greased or non-stick baking tray. Score the top lightly with the blade of a knife. Mix egg yolk with water and brush over the surface. Bake at 180°C for 10–15 minutes until puffed up and golden brown. Cool on a wire rack. Trim asparagus to uniform size and peel the ends of the stems. Cook until just tender in boiling water for 3–4 minutes. Drain and serve the spears sandwiched between the pastry rectangles with a generous serving of blender lemon hollandaise (see page 18).

Fresh asparagus in puff pastry with lemon hollandaise

Parmesan pesto picnic pies

Makes 12

Traditionally bacon and egg pies are very popular for picnics. These are a quicker variation on the theme. They're easy to handle and look like you've gone to a lot of extra trouble by making individual servings, whereas they're actually easier to make. A wonderful lunchtime dish and a great vehicle for any leftovers you find in the fridge.

3 sheets frozen flaky pastry, thawed

1 cup (approx) parmesan cheese, grated

4–5 gherkins or pickled onions, finely chopped

2 tablespoons parsley, finely chopped

2 cups cream

2 tablespoons prepared pesto

6 eggs

extra chopped parsley, to garnish

Pre-heat oven to 200°C. With a large cookie cutter press out circles of pastry approximately 12 cm diameter and press into deep non-stick muffin tins, don't worry if pastry overlaps a little. Sprinkle a few shreds of grated parmesan cheese into the base of each case (this waterproofs the bases), then divide gherkins or pickled onions between the cases. Add salt and pepper and parsley. Beat cream, pesto and eggs together and pour a little into each case, being careful not to overfill. Top each pie with a few shreds of grated parmesan cheese. Bake approximately 25 minutes, until golden and puffed up, with the egg filling set. Ease out the pies from the muffin tins as soon as they are cool enough to handle. These are best served warm sprinkled with fresh parsley.

Variations
* chopped ham or bacon
* finely shredded spinach and feta cheese
* red onion and chopped fresh herbs
* blue cheese and walnuts
* smoked fish and a little horseradish cream
* mussels or any shellfish with a little chopped parsley
* diced red, green and yellow capsicum and chilli flakes

Parmesan pesto picnic pies

Frittata
Serves 4–6

Any combination of vegetables may be used — zucchini and pumpkin are particularly good. A frittata is a good way of dealing with the loaves and fishes dilemma when you appear to have an empty fridge but company has arrived. I've even plumped mine out with cooked rice or left-over pasta.

1 tablespoon oil

4 rashers of rindless bacon, chopped into small pieces

1 large onion, finely chopped

2 cloves garlic, crushed (1 teaspoon)

3 medium potatoes, scrubbed or peeled if desired and diced into
    1 cm pieces

1 cup (approx) button mushrooms, sliced

1 small red capsicum, de-seeded and finely chopped

2–3 tablespoons parsley, chopped

salt and freshly ground black pepper

2 cups cheese, grated (reserve ½ cup for sprinkling over top)

6 large eggs

¼ cup cream (or milk)

Heat the oil in a medium frypan, preferably non-stick, and fry the bacon until brown and crisp. Add the onion, garlic and potato cubes and stir-fry until the potato is soft — about 5–6 minutes. Add the mushrooms, capsicum and parsley. Season with salt and pepper to taste then stir in the grated cheese. In a separate bowl beat the eggs and cream together then pour over the mixture. Turn the heat down to low and cook for about 4 minutes until the bottom is golden crisp and the centre is setting. The top should still be rather wet and uncooked. Remove pan from the heat, sprinkle the reserved grated cheese over the top and place under a grill to brown for 3–4 minutes. Cut into wedges and serve immediately.

Camembert, tomato and zucchini tart

Serves 4

2 sheets pre-rolled puff pastry

200 g camembert

4–5 large plum or Italian tomatoes

3-4 medium-sized zucchini

2 tablespoons olive oil

1 tablespoon chopped fresh basil (or 1 teaspoon dried)

lots freshly ground black pepper

Pre-heat oven to 200°C. Join 2 puff pastry sheets together forming a rectangle and place on a baking sheet. Mark with a knife 2.5 cm from the edge on all sides. Prick the base with a fork inside the marks. Cut the camembert into long, thin slices. Cut tomatoes and zucchini into long, thin slices. In a frying pan, heat 2 tablespoons of olive oil and fry the zucchini for 1–2 minutes until softened. Starting from one end, arrange four overlapping rows of camembert, tomatoes and zucchini within the cut marks. Sprinkle over the basil and season. Bake for 25–30 minutes until the pastry is puffed up and the zucchini are tender. Serve warm.

Thai beef salad
Serves 4

¼ cup oil

2 pieces sirloin steak (approx 500 g)

1 small lettuce

12 cherry tomatoes, halved

1 telegraph cucumber, cut into chunks

4 spring onions, finely sliced

½ cup fresh coriander leaves

Dressing

2 tablespoons Thai fish sauce

2 tablespoons lime juice

2 tablespoons light soy sauce

1 tablespoon sweet chilli sauce

3 cloves garlic, crushed (1 teaspoon)

freshly ground black pepper

Heat the oil in a heavy frypan. Add the steak and cook for about 4 minutes on each side. Remove steak from pan and allow to cool, then slice into thin strips.

To make dressing, in a small bowl mix together all ingredients until well combined.

Arrange the lettuce on a plate with tomatoes, cucumber, spring onion and strips of steak. Drizzle the dressing over the salad and garnish with fresh coriander leaves. Serve immediately.

Roast pear, blue cheese and toasted walnut salad with balsamic dressing

Serves 4

firm green pears (allow ½ a pear per serving)

olive oil

lettuce and selection of salad leaves

soft blue cheese (eg. blue castello or blue brie)

toasted walnuts: 3–4 per serving (50 g approx for 4)

croutons and crispy bacon (optional)

balsamic dressing, 1 tablespoon dressing per serving, see page 111

Peel and core the pears, drizzle with olive oil and roast in a hot oven 200°C for 20–25 minutes until golden and soft. Fill four individual bowls with a selection of lettuce and salad leaves. Slice pear and blue cheese and divide among the bowls. Add walnuts, croutons and crispy bacon if desired and sprinkle with dressing. Serve immediately.

Roast pear, blue cheese and toasted walnut salad with balsamic dressing

Smoked fish and summer vegetable salad
Serves 4–6

4 eggs, hard boiled

1 handful French beans, topped and tailed

2 roasted red peppers (Kato brand, vacuum-packed in olive oil)

1 cup black olives, stoned

2 cups (approx) cherry tomatoes, halved

smoked fish fillets (approx 2 cupfuls)

1 small iceberg or cos lettuce, washed and shaken dry

Dressing

2 spring onions, finely chopped

1 teaspoon red-wine vinegar

1 teaspoon clear honey

large pinch mustard powder

2 tablespoons flat-leaf parsley, freshly chopped

1 tablespoon marjoram, freshly chopped

6 tablespoons olive oil

Peel off shells and quarter the eggs. Blanch the beans for 2 minutes and drain, cutting any large beans in half so that they are easier to eat. In a large bowl carefully mix together the eggs, beans, peppers, olives and tomatoes. Skin and coarsely flake the fish fillets and add to the bowl. Tear any large lettuce leaves and arrange in a serving bowl. Spoon the smoked fish/vegetable mixture on top. Put all the dressing ingredients together in a screw-topped jar with salt and freshly ground black pepper. Screw on the lid and shake until well emulsified, drizzle over the fish mixture and toss together gently.

Smoked fish and summer vegetable salad

Chicken pesto tortellini

Serves 4

2 tablespoons oil

1 double chicken breast, skinned, boned and sliced into thin strips

450 g packet of tortellini (or substitute ravioli)

¼ cup Italian parsley, roughly chopped

½ cup prepared pesto sauce

½ cup cream

shaved parmesan

4–6 cherry tomatoes, sliced in half

In frypan, heat oil and add chicken, stir-fry for 8–10 minutes. Cook pasta in large saucepan of boiling water as per instructions on the packet. Drain well, reserving 1 cup of pasta water. Mix together cooked chicken, pasta, chopped parsley, pesto and cream. Add a little reserved pasta water to extend the sauce if necessary. Serve garnished with fresh parmesan cheese and halved cherry tomatoes.

Chicken pesto tortellini

Pumpkin and feta fritter with peanut sauce

Makes about 10 fritters

4 eggs

1 cup self-raising flour

1 cup pumpkin, grated or finely chopped, microwaved or steamed
   until just softened

2–3 cloves garlic, crushed (1 teaspoon)

½ cup feta cheese, finely chopped or crumbled

½ cup parsley, chopped

freshly ground black pepper

¼ cup oil and 50 g butter, to cook

In a bowl beat eggs. Mix in flour to a smooth batter (can be done in a food processor or with an electric mixer). Add pumpkin, garlic, feta, parsley, pepper (remember the feta is quite salty so probably no extra salt is required). Heat oil and butter in a pan over medium heat until butter has melted and is bubbly. Spoon a large tablespoon per fritter, cooking 2–3 fritters at a time, and fry for approximately 3 minutes. Then carefully turn and cook the other side. Drain on paper towels and keep warm while you fry remaining mixture.

Peanut sauce

1 cup (approx) crunchy peanut butter

1 teaspoon crushed ginger

1 tablespoon sweet chilli sauce

1 tablespoon fresh lemon juice

1½ cups coconut cream (or cream)

Mix together over gentle heat until warmed through and blended. Serve with fritters, satays, barbecued steaks, etc.

*Pumpkin and feta fritter
with peanut sauce*

Chicken caesar salad

Serves 4

1 tablespoon olive oil

1 double chicken breast, skin and bones removed

1 cos lettuce, well washed and broken into leaves

3 rashers bacon, chopped and cooked crisp in the oven

4 slices French bread, toasted and cut into small croutons

½ cup parmesan shavings, plus extra to garnish

2 eggs, hard boiled and sliced

Dressing

2–4 anchovies, chopped

2 egg yolks

2 tablespoons white-wine vinegar

2–3 cloves garlic, crushed (1 teaspoon)

2 teaspoon Dijon mustard

1 cup olive oil

2 tablespoons parsley, chopped

Heat oil in frypan. Cook chicken breasts for 4 minutes on each side until cooked through. Remove from pan and slice into strips. Fill four bowls with cos lettuce leaves and add chicken strips, crispy bacon, toasted French bread croutons, parmesan cheese and hard-boiled eggs.

To make dressing, mix together the anchovies, egg yolks, white-wine vinegar, garlic and mustard in a food processor or bowl until smooth. Add the oil slowly, in a thin stream, until the dressing is thick and creamy, add chopped parsley. Drizzle over the salad, sprinkle with extra parmesan and serve.

The main
event

Pasta wraps with chicken and prosciutto

Serves 4–6

- 3 cups shaved parmesan cheese
- 2 cups cooked shredded chicken
- 6–8 slices prosciutto
- 1 packet fresh lasagne sheets (4–5 sheets)
- 3 cloves garlic, crushed (1 teaspoon)
- 300 ml cream or tomato juice
- 2 x 400 g cans chopped tomatoes in juice (or crushed tomatoes and onion)
- ½ cup white wine
- 2 cups sliced button mushrooms
- 1 cup mozzarella cheese, grated
- tomato, parsley and basil, to garnish

Place a handful of cheese and chicken and approximately one slice of prosciutto on top of a pasta sheet, covering all but a couple of centimetres in from the edge. Roll up the pasta sheet tightly and repeat with remaining pasta. Cut each pasta roll into 3 or 4 pieces and place in a baking dish, layering the rolls as necessary. Place garlic and cream in a large frypan, stir over medium heat, add the tomatoes, wine and mushrooms, then bring to the boil. Pour over the pasta rolls and sprinkle the top with mozzarella cheese. Bake at 180°C for 30 minutes. Remove from oven and garnish the top with chopped fresh tomato, Italian parsley and basil.

Pasta wraps with chicken prosciutto

Baked tuna and penne
Serves 4

50 g butter

2 tablespoons flour

1 teaspoon dry mustard powder

1½ cups milk

2 teaspoons lemon juice

1 x 185 g can tuna, drained and flaked

2 cups penne pasta (or macaroni), cooked and drained

1 cup cheese, grated

salt and freshly ground black pepper

In a saucepan melt butter, stir in flour and cook for 1 minute. Add mustard powder, milk and lemon juice and stir for 5 minutes until sauce begins to boil and thicken. Stir in tuna, penne pasta, half the cheese and salt and freshly ground black pepper to taste. Transfer to small lasagne or pie dish. Sprinkle with remaining cheese. Bake at 180°C for 20 minutes until cheese melts and the top is all golden brown.

Baked tuna and penne

Duck breasts with mushroom pumpkin risotto

Serves 4

100 g butter

2 medium onions, chopped

3 cloves garlic, crushed (1 teaspoon)

1½ cups risotto (arborio) rice

500 g (approx 4 cups) pumpkin, peeled, deseeded and cut into
  1 cm cubes

juice and grated rind of 1 orange, plus extra peel for garnish

600 ml hot chicken stock

3 cups (250 g) mixed fancy mushrooms, sliced

1 cup (approx) shaved fresh parmesan cheese, reserve a little as
  garnish

4 single duck breasts

4 tablespoons chutney or relish of your choice

salt and freshly ground black pepper

Heat butter in a large sauté or deep frypan. Add the onion and garlic and cook until onion is soft and transparent. Add the arborio rice then the pumpkin, and sauté over gentle heat for 6–8 minutes, until the pumpkin is just beginning to soften. Add the orange juice and grated rind. Stir to mix well. Turn heat up slightly to medium and add the hot chicken stock, a little at a time, stirring constantly allowing the liquid to be absorbed after each addition. This will take 20–25 minutes. Finally, add the mushrooms and freshly shaved parmesan cheese. Stir to mix well. The rice should be tender but firm to the bite and creamily bound together.

While the rice is cooking, score duck breast through fat, being careful not to cut into the meat. Rub with salt and pepper and roast at 200°C for approximately 20 minutes, until crispy and cooked through — don't overcook.

Serve duck breast on the risotto with a chutney of your choice (such as Kato Roast Plum Thai Chutney). Garnish the dish with shaved parmesan and extra finely shredded orange peel.

Duck breasts with mushroom pumpkin risotto

Braised pork chops with prunes and apricots

Serves 4

4 trimmed meaty pork chops

salt and freshly ground black pepper

¼ cup flour

¼ cup oil

2–3 cloves garlic, crushed (1 teaspoon)

2 large onions, sliced

4 cups chicken or beef stock

2 cups red wine

12 (approx) pitted prunes

12 (approx) dried apricots

Season pork with salt and pepper. Place flour on a plate or in a shallow dish and season with salt and more pepper. Coat the pork in the flour, shaking off the excess. Heat oil in a heavy oven-proof pan. Add pork and cook a few minutes on each side to brown. Remove pork and drain off oil leaving approximately 2 tablespoons. Add garlic and onions and sauté for 3–4 minutes until golden. Return chops to the pan. Add stock, wine and dried fruit. Place in the oven at 180°C for approximately 45 minutes or simmer until pork is tender. Remove pork to serving dish. Bring the remaining liquid to the boil, reducing if necessary, until thickened and 'sauce like'. Check seasoning and pour sauce evenly over pork chops.

Braised pork chops with prunes and apricots

Individual pork and apple meatloaves wrapped in bacon

Serves 4

1 tablespoon oil

1 medium onion, finely chopped

2–3 cloves garlic, crushed (1 teaspoon)

2 cups fresh white breadcrumbs

800 g minced pork

2 eggs, beaten

1 cup thick stewed apple (or canned apple pie filling)

2 tablespoons wholegrain mustard

1 tablespoon tomato sauce

2 teaspoons sweet chilli sauce

1 tablespoon parsley, finely chopped

1 tablespoon chives, finely sliced

salt and freshly ground black pepper

8 rashers rindless bacon

Heat oil in a small pan and stir-fry onion until softened. Add garlic and breadcrumbs and cook 2 minutes. Mix mince with onion mixture then bind together with beaten eggs, apple, mustard, tomato and chilli sauces, parsley and chives. Season with salt and freshly ground black pepper. With wet hands form mince into 4 little meatloaves, then wrap 2 bacon rashers around each loaf and place in an oiled roasting dish. Bake in a pre-heated 200°C oven for about 30–35 minutes, until the bacon is crisp and the meatloaves are cooked right through. These are splendid served with grainy mustard sauce, super garlicky mashed potatoes and steamed green vegetables.

Grainy mustard sauce

250 g sour cream or lite sour cream

2 tablespoons wholegrain mustard

2 tablespoons parsley, chopped

Mix together all the ingredients in a small bowl. Serve at room temperature.

Individual pork and apple meatloaves wrapped in bacon

Crying leg of lamb with roasted vegetables

Serves 4–6

potatoes, kumara, lemons — cut into thin slices, figs, parsnip, baby
onions, spring onions, pumpkin, mushrooms, radishes

1.5 kg leg lamb on the bone

10 cloves garlic

2 tablespoons oil

Lemon rosemary topping

finely grated rind of three lemons

2 tablespoons fresh rosemary leaves, chopped

4 tablespoons parsley, chopped

salt and freshly ground black pepper

Pre-heat oven to 200°C. Trim, peel and prepare the vegetables and fruit, keeping pieces of root vegetables a uniform size. Remove skin from lamb, leaving a thin layer of fat. Peel garlic cloves and slice in half. Cut slashes in lamb fat and push a garlic slice into each one. Sprinkle the topping over the lamb. Place vegetables in bottom of roasting pan with 2 tablespoons of oil to prevent sticking, and place lamb on a rack above the vegetables. Roast in the oven for 1 hour 20 minutes. The lamb is cooked when the juices that run out of the meat when pierced with a skewer are faintly pink. Rest lamb out of oven at least 10 minutes before carving. Serve with redcurrant, mint or rosehip jelly.

Fish fillets with parmesan lemon crumb crust

Serves 4

4 fish fillets, skinned and boned (terakihi, snapper, wild trout, cod, etc)

juice and rind 2 lemons

salt and freshly ground black pepper

½ cup fresh breadcrumbs (whiz 2 slices of thick toast-cut bread in the food processor)

½ cup parmesan cheese, grated

¼ cup fresh herbs, chopped (parsley, dill, tarragon, chives, etc)

50 g butter

Remove all or as many bones from the fish fillets as possible and place in a greased baking dish. Finely grate the lemon rind and toss this with salt and pepper, the breadcrumbs, parmesan and herbs. Press this crumb mixture into the top side of the fish fillets. Melt the butter and add the squeezed lemon juice, then pour over the crumbed fish and bake in a pre-heated oven at 220°C for 12–15 minutes or place under the grill for 6–8 minutes.

Bourbon beef stroganoff with jasmine rice

Serves 4

2 tablespoons oil

2 medium onions, sliced

large fillet of beef (depending on size, about 700 g), cut into strips
like French fries

250 g (approx 3 cups) button mushrooms, sliced

salt and freshly ground black pepper

½ cup bourbon

3 tablespoons grainy mustard

250 g sour cream

Heat the oil in a large frypan, add onions and stir-fry until starting to caramelise golden brown. Remove from pan and add the beef, then stir-fry over a high heat until brown. Add onions back to the pan with the mushrooms. Season with salt and lots of pepper, add bourbon and stir for 3 minutes. Lower heat and stir in the mustard and sour cream. Let the sauce bubble and reduce down. Serve immediately over jasmine rice or buttered noodles.

To cook jasmine rice, bring 2 litres of water to the boil, then add ½ teaspoon of salt and stir in 1 cup of jasmine or fragrant rice. Bring the pot back to the boil and simmer uncovered for 12 minutes. Drain and serve.

*Bourbon beef
stroganoff with
jasmine rice*

Perfect roast fillet of beef

Serves 4–6

Ask your butcher to cut your beef trimmed of all sinew and fat and the same thickness throughout without any thin ends or scrappy pieces attached

1 eye fillet of beef

salt and freshly ground black pepper

Pre-heat oven to 220°C. Place the meat in a roasting dish and season generously with salt and pepper. Place in the hot oven, quickly close the door so as not to let too much heat out. Time for exactly 20 minutes — not 19 and not 22 — but bang on 20! When the buzzer of the timer goes off, remove the roasting dish and cover meat with tinfoil (like a little tent). Rest the meat for 10–12 minutes like this before serving. This stops the meat 'bleeding' everywhere — the juices are brought to the meat's surface when it's cooking and resting it allows the juices to soak back into the meat, keeping it tender and moist. The 20-minute rule always works for tender, perfect, pink-but-not-bloody beef.

Perfect pan-roasted fillet steaks

Pan-roasting is a simple technique that involves searing the food on top of the stove, then completing the cooking in a hot oven. Pan-roasting gives a crisp crust and juicy interior to tender cuts of meat, poultry and thick pieces of fish.

Fillet steaks, sliced into 4–5cm thick pieces (allowing 1–2 per person depending on the appetite of big rugby playing chaps or more dainty eaters)

Lightly oil a pan and fry steaks over a high heat to brown and sear the surface on both sides, then finish by placing the pan in a hot 220°C oven. (Make sure the handle is oven-proof.) Roast for 4 minutes for medium-rare, a little longer, say 5–6 minutes, for more well done. Remove from oven, cover pan with tinfoil, like a tent, and rest the meat for 5–10 minutes to prevent the juices bleeding.

Creamy chicken potatoes Dijon

Serves 4

A quick, easy and very impressive dinner dish.

6 medium potatoes

1 tablespoon olive oil

25g butter

1 small onion, finely chopped

2–3 cloves garlic, crushed (1 teaspoon)

2 double chicken breasts, boneless, skinless and sliced into thin strips

1 tablespoon parsley, chopped

1 cup cream

1 tablespoon Dijon mustard

salt and freshly ground black pepper

½ cup tasty cheese

Pre-heat oven to 200°C. Grease a shallow ovenproof dish. Slice potatoes thinly, then boil in a saucepan of boiling water for 10 minutes until just tender. Heat oil and butter in a frypan, add onion and garlic and fry for 3–4 minutes until softened. Add chicken and fry until browned. Stir in the parsley, cream and mustard then season well with salt and pepper. Spread half the potatoes in the dish. Spoon over the chicken mixture, cover with remaining potatoes. Sprinkle the top with cheese. Bake for 20–25 minutes until crisp and golden. Serve with green salad.

Grilled salmon with blender lemon hollandaise

Serves 4

Salmon

4 salmon fillets, with skin on but carefully remove any bones
(tweezers work well for this task)

salt and freshly ground black pepper

(optional: 2 tablespoons grated cheese that has also been chopped
extra fine with a knife to resemble breadcrumbs)

Pre-heat oven to 200°C. Line a large baking sheet with tinfoil, spray with non-stick olive oil spray. Arrange salmon on foil and again spray the salmon fillets with olive oil and season with salt and pepper. Bake for about 15 minutes, until just cooked through (for the optional cheese topping: lightly sprinkle with the finely chopped grated cheese, this will be golden and crispy over the surface of the salmon). Transfer to serving plates and serve the sauce (see page 18) alongside. Garnish with fresh chives.

*Grilled salmon with
blender lemon
hollandaise*

Cumin lemon chicken with chickpeas

Serves 4

juice and grated rind of 1 lemon

1 teaspoon ground cumin

4 tablespoons olive oil

salt and freshly ground black pepper

4 skinless boneless chicken breasts

5 (1 bunch) spring onions, finely sliced

2–3 cloves garlic, crushed (1 teaspoon)

1 teaspoon paprika

2 x 400 g can chickpeas, drained

½ teaspoon sugar

3 tablespoons parsley, chopped

In a bowl mix together half the lemon juice, all the cumin, 1 tablespoon of the oil, salt and pepper, then roll the chicken in the mixture to coat. Heat 1 tablespoon oil in a frypan and cook the chicken for 4–5 minutes on each side until golden and cooked through.

In a separate pan, briefly cook the spring onions, garlic and paprika in the remaining oil without browning. Stir in the chickpeas, grated lemon rind and gently warm through.

Add the remaining lemon juice, 2–3 tablespoons water and sugar to the pan with the chicken and let it bubble. Serve the chicken and juices with the chickpeas and garnish with parsley. Serve with a green salad.

*Cumin lemon chicken
with chickpeas*

Cajun spiced oven-baked fish fillets with mango salsa
Serves 4

4 fresh fish fillets (or 2 large ones cut in half — snapper, orange roughy, terakihi, etc)

olive oil spray

juice of ½ lemon or lime

1– 2 teaspoons Cajun spice mix

Heat oven to 200°C. Place fish fillets in an oil-sprayed baking dish, tucking thin ends underneath so the fish fillets are of equal thickness.

Spray fish with olive oil and squeeze over lemon (or lime) juice. Sprinkle with Cajun spice and bake for 10–12 minutes until cooked through. Serve fish with mango salsa and extra wedges of lemon or lime, with crispy oven fries and a green vegetable, such as steamed beans or courgette.

Mango salsa
Serves 4–6

2 mangoes, peeled, cored and cut into similar-sized dice (or 1 x 425 g can of mangoes in natural juice)

½ small red onion or sweet onion, finely chopped

½ small red pepper, de-seeded and finely chopped

1 tablespoon sweet chilli sauce

¼ cup freshly squeezed lime or lemon juice

1 teaspoon lemon or lime rind, grated

2 tablespoons extra virgin olive oil

½ cup (approx) fresh coriander, chopped

salt and freshly ground black pepper

Place all ingredients in a large bowl and toss to mix well. Season with salt and pepper and chill. Best to eat within 2 to 3 hours of making.

Cajun spiced oven-baked fish fillets with mango salsa

Peanut tandoori chicken with fresh coriander

Serves 4

2 double chicken breasts, skin and bones removed

3 tablespoons (approx) tandoori paste (available in jars from
supermarkets and delicatessens)

2 tablespoons oil

1 tablespoon white-wine vinegar

½ cup crunchy peanut butter

250 g (approx 3 cups) button mushrooms, sliced

½ cup (approx) parsley, chopped

½ cup fresh coriander, chopped

500 g (2 cups) sour cream or thick natural yoghurt or a mixture
of both

extra chopped parsley and coriander, to garnish

Cut up chicken into bite-size-pieces and place in a casserole dish. Mix tandoori paste with oil and white-wine vinegar and stir into chicken, coating well. Leave covered in fridge for at least 3–4 hours (preferably overnight).

In a large frying pan, cook chicken over a medium heat for 10–15 minutes, stirring. When cooked through, add peanut butter, mushrooms, parsley, coriander and half of the sour cream or yoghurt. Simmer for 15 minutes. Just before serving, stir in the remaining sour cream or yoghurt, mix well to blend in and sprinkle with extra herbs to garnish. Serve immediately with couscous (see page 106), rice or buttered noodles.

*Peanut tandoori chicken
with fresh coriander*

Ginger chicken breasts wrapped in bacon with couscous and apricot yoghurt sauce

Serves 4

2 teaspoons fresh ginger, grated

1 tablespoon soft butter or margarine

1 tablespoon parsley, chopped

4 single boneless chicken breasts with skin on

4 long rashers of streaky rindless bacon

garlic salt

Apricot yoghurt sauce

1 cup (approx) or a small can apricots in fruit juice, puréed or well mashed

1 cup (150 g) plain natural yoghurt

2–3 cloves garlic, crushed (1 teaspoon)

1 teaspoon sweet chilli sauce

3 tablespoons parsley, chopped

Mix ginger, butter or margarine and parsley until well combined. Spread mixture on the underside of the chicken breasts. Wrap each breast skin side up in a figure 8 fashion with the rashers of bacon. Place on a baking tray and sprinkle with garlic salt. Bake at 180°C for 25–30 minutes until the bacon and chicken skin are crisp and golden. Serve with couscous (see page 106) or rice and apricot yoghurt sauce.

To make sauce, mix all sauce ingredients together and serve at room temperature spooned over chicken.

Vegetables, side dishes and dressings

Parmesan polenta
Serves 4–6

4 cups of well-flavoured chicken stock or vegetable stock

salt and pepper

1½ cups polenta cornmeal

1 cup parmesan cheese, grated

Bring the stock to the boil, adding salt and pepper to taste. Pour the polenta into the boiling stock in a steady flow while you stir continuously. Turn down heat to a very gentle simmer for about 10 minutes. Stir until polenta is thick and smooth and pulls away from the edges of the saucepan. Stir in the parmesan cheese. The polenta can now be eaten in this basic form as an alternative to potatoes or pasta.

To fry polenta, follow the method above but pour about 1 cm thick into a plastic wrap or foil-lined tray and leave for an hour or so to set and cool. Slice into thick toast-like pieces and fry in hot oil for a few minutes until golden brown. Alternatively sprinkle the toast-like slices with grated parmesan and grill on each side until a crisp brown crust forms.

Couscous

Use 1½ cups of water or chicken stock to a cup of dry couscous. Boil water or chicken stock. Add 1 tablespoon olive oil and salt to taste for each cup of couscous. When water is boiling, turn off heat, add couscous. Wait 2 minutes for liquid to be absorbed then fluff up couscous with a fork. Couscous can be flavoured with sweet chilli sauce or chilli powder, fresh herbs, seasoning mixtures (cajun spice, cinnamon, etc), crushed garlic, lemon or orange juice and finely grated zest. Be creative with the flavouring as it can be quite bland without 'help'. Cold couscous makes a great salad ingredient and can be easily reheated or microwaved.

Roast vegetables

Serves 4–6

A variety of vegetables are suitable for roasting, such as carrots, parsnips, pumpkin, whole radishes, kumara, yellow and red peppers and artichokes, garlic cloves and, of course, potatoes.

½ pumpkin

1 large kumara

8 small onions

3 tablespoons olive oil

Pre-heat oven to 200°C. Peel the pumpkin and kumara and cut into large pieces. Peel the onions but leave whole. Pour the oil into a large baking dish. Put in the oven to heat the oil. Add the vegetables to the dish and toss to coat with the hot oil. Bake for 45–50 minutes, or until the vegetables are crisp, golden and cooked through. Turn occasionally during cooking to coat with the oil and prevent sticking. Drain excess oil on paper towels before serving.

Simple speedy cauliflower cheese

Bring small florets of cauliflower to the boil and cook briefly (just 2–3 minutes until tender). Drain and place in a grill-proof dish. Season with salt and freshly ground black pepper and dollop over a thin layer of sour cream and sprinkle generously with grated tasty cheese or parmesan cheese. Place under a hot grill for 2–3 minutes until the cheese is bubbly and golden brown.

Super garlicky mashed potatoes

Serves 4

1 kg 'Red Rascal' or floury potatoes, peeled (these are ideal to mash)

2 tablespoons olive oil

50 g butter

10–12 cloves garlic, crushed (3 teaspoons approx)

¼ cup (possibly more) milk

salt and freshly ground black pepper

Cut up and cook potatoes in boiling water for 15–20 minutes until tender, then drain in colander. Into the potato saucepan heat oil and butter and soften crushed garlic for 2–3 minutes, then add milk. When milk is warm, return potatoes to the pot and mash with extra milk as required. Season with salt and pepper.

Crispy garlic roast potatoes and onions

1 medium-sized potato per person

1 medium-sized onion per person

oil, for coating

garlic salt

rosemary or parsley, chopped

Scrub potatoes, do not peel, and chop roughly into 2 cm cubes. Peel and cut onions into quarters then eighths, like orange segments. Place onions and cubed potatoes in a roasting dish, sprinkle with oil so that they are lightly coated, then dust with garlic salt. Roast in a medium-hot oven at 180°C for 25–30 minutes until crispy and golden. Toss in chopped rosemary or parsley before serving.

Crispy garlic roast potatoes and onions

Crispy potato parmesan cake

Serves 4–6

50 g butter

2 medium-sized onions, finely chopped

6 potatoes, medium size

1 cup parmesan cheese, grated

3 eggs

½ cup milk (or cream)

salt and pepper

extra 50 g butter

Melt the butter in a frying pan, and gently fry the onions for approximately 10 minutes until golden brown. While the onion is frying, peel the potatoes and grate coarsely. Wash off the excess starch in a large bowl of cold water. Drain and wring dry in a tea towel. Add the cooked onion and butter to the potato. Separate the eggs, and add the yolks to the potato mixture, together with the milk or cream and parmesan cheese. Season well with salt and pepper. Whisk the egg whites until they form soft peaks, and fold in. Pile the mixture into a greased, watertight 21 cm spring tin. Dot with the extra butter and bake at 180°C for about 40 minutes, until the top is golden brown and crispy and the potatoes tender in the centre.

Baby beetroot with sour cream

A quick vegetable idea from the store cupboard. Drain a can of baby beetroots. Microwave to warm, then drizzle over sour cream or natural yoghurt and sprinkle with chopped parsley and ground black pepper.

Salad dressings

Mayonnaise

3 egg yolks

2 teaspoons white-wine vinegar

1 tablespoon smooth Dijon mustard

200 ml olive oil

200 ml vegetable oil

2 tablespoons hot water

salt and freshly ground black pepper

In food processor or blender mix egg yolks, white-wine vinegar and mustard. With machine running, slowly drizzle in olive and vegetable oil. Whisk in 2 tablespoons hot water to stabilise mayonnaise. Season to taste.

Basic vinaigrette

½ cup extra virgin olive oil

2 tablespoons white-wine vinegar

1 teaspoon sugar

1 teaspoon of prepared smooth Dijon mustard

salt and freshly ground black pepper

Place all ingredients into a screw-top jar and shake vigorously until well blended and season with salt and pepper.

Balsamic dressing

½ cup extra virgin olive oil

2 tablespoon balsamic vinegar

1 teaspoon honey

salt and freshly ground black pepper

Place all ingredients into a screw-top jar and shake vigorously until well blended.

Asian dressing

- 1 tablespoon Thai fish sauce (available in supermarkets and delicatessens)
- 2 tablespoons sweet chilli sauce
- 2 tablespoons fresh lime juice
- ½ teaspoon garlic, crushed
- ¼ cup peanut oil
- 1 tablespoon toasted sesame oil
- 1 tablespoon fresh coriander, chopped

Place all ingredients into a small bowl. Whisk together until well combined.

Breads and baking

Pizza dough to make in the food processor

Makes 2 large pizzas

1 teaspoon sugar

1 cup warm water

1 teaspoon active dry yeast granules

3 cups flour

1 teaspoon salt

¼ cup olive oil

Place the sugar, warm water and yeast in the food processor and leave for 10–15 minutes until the mixture is frothy. Add the flour, salt and oil and process to form a soft dough that pulls away in a lump from the blade. Tip onto a floured bench and knead until soft and silky. Place the dough in an oiled bowl and cover with plastic wrap. Leave in a warm place to rise until doubled in size. Unwrap, then punch the dough down and knead for a further 2–3 minutes. Break off pieces the size of tennis balls. Roll out into circles and add your favourite pizza topping: tomato, anchovy, olive, salami, ham, pineapple, cheese, etc . . . Cook pizza at 200°C fanbake for 10 minutes.

A calzone is a folded-over pizza with the filling on the inside. Brush or spray the surface of the calzone with oil before baking for a lovely glossy golden crust.

Focaccia bread
(The food processor variety)

1 tablespoon dried yeast granules

1½ cups warm water

½ teaspoon sugar

4½ cups flour

½ cup olive oil

1 teaspoon salt

rock or sea salt, rosemary

In food processor mix yeast, water and sugar. When frothy, add flour, oil and salt. Run machine until dough is smooth and non-sticky. Place in oiled bowl covered with plastic cling wrap. Leave to rise until doubled in bulk, approximately 1 hour.

Knead on floured bench, then flatten in a well-oiled roasting dish to 2 cm thick. Cover and leave to rise again until doubled in size. Make indentations in the top with finger tips and brush with oil. Sprinkle with salt and rosemary as desired. Bake at 220°C for 15 minutes then reduce heat to 200°C. Cook for a further 25–30 minutes, then cool.

Focaccia bread

Beer bread

This is one of my signature recipes and I couldn't possibly leave it out. It's a wonderfully quick bread that has the texture, taste and best of all the smell of a lovely fresh-from-the-oven farmhouse loaf.

3 cups flour

3 teaspoons baking powder

1 teaspoon salt

1 can beer (approximately 400 ml, just rinse out the can with water
     to make up the volume) don't use low-alcohol beer

1 handful (about ½ cup) grated cheese

Pre-heat the oven to 200°C. Mix flour, baking powder, salt and beer in a large bowl until well combined. Tip into 1 large 21 x 12 cm non-stick or well-greased loaf tin (alternatively use two 8 cm x 15 cm small tins). Sprinkle the top with grated cheese. Bake the large loaf for 50–60 minutes or the two little loaves for 30–40 minutes until golden brown. Tip out and cool on a wire rack before slicing. This bread keeps well and also makes excellent toast.

Featherweight cheese puffs

Makes about 12

3 cups grated cheese

2 cups flour

4 teaspoons baking powder

2 eggs

¾ cup milk

Pre-heat oven to 240°C (the hottest the oven will heat to). Mix all ingredients together in a large bowl. Drop spoonfuls of mixture onto a well-greased or non-stick oven tray and place in the hot oven immediately. Make sure you close the oven door as quickly as possible then turn the oven off. Bake for 10 minutes. Remove from oven and cool on a wire rack. Serve warm.

Featherweight
cheese puffs

Scones

The lemonade method for ultra-quick scones in a jiff. I've even served these with fresh strawberries for dessert.

4 cups self-raising flour

300 ml (1 carton or small bottle) cream

1 can (355 ml) lemonade

½ teaspoon salt

Mix all ingredients in a bowl to a smooth dough. Tip out onto a well-floured surface and cut into squares or press out with a scone cutter. Bake at 220°C (fanbake if you have it) for about 15–20 minutes until starting to colour golden. Check they are cooked through and cool on a wire rack.

Serve warm with jam or whole fruit preserves and whipped cream, garnish with fresh fruit as desired.

Chocolate-chunk oat cookies

250 g butter

3 tablespoons condensed milk

¾ cup sugar

1 ½ cups flour

1 ½ cups rolled oats

1 teaspoon baking powder

250 g dark chocolate, chopped

Beat butter, condensed milk and sugar together until light and creamy. Add flour, rolled oats, baking powder and chocolate pieces. Put dessertspoonfuls of mixture onto a greased oven tray and flatten with a fork. Cook at 170°C for 20 minutes until golden brown.

Peanut butter biscuits

2 cups (about 800 g or ½ a big jar) crunchy peanut butter

2 cups sugar

2 eggs

Mix ingredients until well combined. Drop spoonfuls onto a greased tray and flatten with a fork. Bake at 170°C fanbake (if possible) for 10 minutes.

Chocolate-chunk oat cookies (top) and peanut butter biscuits

Fresh plum cake

This recipe works well with fresh apricots, peaches, apple or plums.
Great for afternoon tea or as a special dessert.

1 cup sugar

juice and grated rind of 1 lemon

200 g butter, softened

3 eggs

150 g (1 tub) yoghurt (plum or vanilla flavours are great or just
    plain yoghurt)

3 cups fresh plums, finely chopped

½ cup chopped nuts (optional)

2 cups flour

3 teaspoons baking powder

1 teaspoon ground cinnamon

icing sugar, for dusting

In a food processor place the sugar and peeled rind of 1 lemon, running the
machine until the rind is finely chopped and incorporated with the sugar
(approx 30 seconds). Add the lemon juice then the butter and mix until
creamy. Add the eggs and mix well. Mix in the yoghurt, fruit, nuts, flour,
baking powder and cinnamon — don't overmix, just combine loosely. Pour
into a well-greased and baking-paper-lined 21 cm cake tin. Bake at 180°C for
55–60 minutes. Cool on a wire rack. Serve dusted with icing sugar and extra
fruit-flavoured yoghurt or softly whipped cream.

Fresh plum cake

Feijoa and orange cake

100 g butter

½ cup sugar

1 tablespoon golden syrup

1 egg

1 teaspoon baking soda

2 tablespoons hot water

1^3/$_4$ cups flour

2 teaspoons baking powder

1 cup (about 6 feijoas) feijoa pulp

juice and grated rind of 1 orange

4 tablespoons demerara sugar

In a food processor or large bowl mix the butter and sugar until creamy. Add the golden syrup and egg. Mix together the baking soda and hot water and add to the mixture. Finally add the flour and baking powder then the feijoa pulp, do not overmix. Pour into a 21 cm cake tin that has been greased and lined with baking paper. Bake at 160°C for 45 minutes. Mix together the grated rind and juice of 1 orange with the demerara sugar and pour over the cake and pop back into the oven for another 15 minutes.

Feijoa and orange
cake

Banana loaf

A great recipe that can be cooked as a loaf, muffins or a cake.

125 g butter

1 cup sugar

2 eggs

2 to 3 bananas, mashed (approx 1 cup)

2 cups flour

1 teaspoon baking powder

1 teaspoon baking soda

In a food processor or large bowl mix together butter and sugar until light and fluffy. Add the egg and mashed bananas, mixing thoroughly. Mix in the flour, baking powder and baking soda, but do not overmix. Pour mixture into a 21 cm cake tin or large loaf tin, well greased and lined on the bottom with baking paper. Bake at 180°C for 45–50 minutes. Cool in tin before turning out onto a wire rack. Can be eaten straight away as a dessert or iced with lemon or cream-cheese frosting.

Desserts

Chocolate mud cake

Serves 8

1½ cups self-raising flour

½ cup plain flour

½ cup cocoa

250 g butter, chopped

1 tablespoon oil

200 g dark chocolate melts (Nestlé)

1½ cups caster sugar

1 cup water

2 eggs, lightly beaten

Ganache topping

300 ml cream

1 packet dark chocolate melts 375 g (Nestlé)

Pre-heat oven to 180°C. Grease a deep 21 cm spring-form tin and line with baking paper. In a large bowl mix together flours and cocoa. In another bowl or saucepan add butter, oil, chocolate, sugar and 1 cup water. Heat over low heat or in the microwave until the chocolate and butter are melted and the sugar has dissolved. Pour into the dry ingredients, add the eggs and whisk until just combined, do not overmix. Pour into the tin and bake for 1½ hours, or until a skewer comes out clean when inserted into the centre of the cake. Leave in the tin to cool completely.

To make ganache topping, in a saucepan stir the cream and chocolate over a low heat until melted. Pour the topping over the cake while still in the tin. Remove from the tin once the topping has set. This cake is delicious served with cream or ice-cream.

Chocolate mud cake

Sticky date pudding

1 ½ cups dates, pitted and chopped

1 teaspoon baking soda

150 ml boiling water

125 g butter

¾ cup sugar

2 eggs

1 heaped cup self-raising flour

Sauce

3 cups loosely packed brown sugar

75 g butter

300 ml cream

1 teaspoon vanilla essence

In a bowl sprinkle the dates with the soda, then pour the boiling water over them. Stir until soda is all dissolved and allow to stand for 10–15 minutes. In a separate bowl, beat butter and sugar until creamy. Add eggs one at a time, beating until light and fluffy. Stir in the flour, the soaked dates and water mixture.

Pour into a deep, well-greased and floured 21 cm cake tin, or deep pie plate. Bake at 190°C for 30–35 minutes or until a skewer inserted into the centre of pudding comes out clean. Allow pudding to stand in tin while you prepare the sauce.

To make sauce, combine all ingredients in a saucepan and stir over a medium heat until sugar is dissolved. Bring to the boil. Turn down and simmer for 5 minutes. Pour a little of the sauce (about 4 tablespoons) over the cooked pudding, then put it back in oven for a few minutes to allow sauce to soak in and bubble to a golden-brown colour. Serve with the extra sauce and whipped cream.

Apricot and blackberry cake-mix crumble

Serves 6

1 large can apricots in syrup or fruit juice (850 g)

3 cups (approx) blackberries, fresh or frozen (sprinkle with sugar
to taste)

1 packet (360 g) cake mix (Edmonds butter cake mix)

100 g butter, melted

Place apricots and half of the juice with blackberries in an ovenproof pie
dish, check for sweetness and sprinkle with sugar if desired. Sprinkle over dry
cake mix and pour over the melted butter. Bake at 180°C for 35 minutes.
Serve with whipped cream or ice-cream.

Strawberry chocolate parfaits

2 cups strawberries, hulled, cut in half and free-flow frozen

¼ cup caster sugar

½ cup cream

½ cup dark chocolate, chopped

Mince frozen berries in a food processor (don't mind the noise). Add sugar and briefly process. With motor on, pour cream into mix through feed tube. Finally add chocolate, but only run machine to mix through. Don't over-process. Serve immediately (refreezing loses texture).

Variations

- Thick yoghurt may be substituted for cream
- Peaches instead of strawberries, peel and cut up before freezing
- Banana instead of strawberries, freeze in their skins then peel and slice
- Blueberries — freeze whole (free flow)

Easy caramel ice-cream

So easy, the only measure you need for the milk and cream is the empty can from the condensed milk.

2 x 400 g cans sweetened condensed milk (caramelised by gently boiling for at least 2 hours in the can)

2 cans milk

2 cans cream, whipped

Mix together all ingredients in a bowl and freeze until firm, 4–6 hours approximately or preferably overnight. (Can be made in an ice-cream machine — no need to whip cream first if using one.)

Caramello/ Moro Bar sauce

1 medium size block (250 g) caramello chocolate

    or (250 g) Moro Bar

½ cup cream

Chop up chocolate or chocolate bars and mix with cream in a small saucepan. Stir over gentle heat until melted and smooth. Serve over ice-cream.

Quick dessert ideas

- Slice beautifully ripe fresh peaches, apricots or nectarines into a stemmed wine glass and drizzle over dessert wine or orange liqueur (cointreau, grand marnier, etc). Garnish with sprigs of mint and, if desired, serve with flavoured yoghurt.

- A mixture of blueberries, strawberries, raspberries and blackberries with a little caster sugar and port is also a great easy dessert. A dark berry or plum yoghurt is a good accompaniment.

- Buy Italian amaretti biscuits (they are often sold in distinctive red tins at delicatessens and the gourmet section of the supermarket). Mix cream cheese with freshly squeezed orange juice and grated orange rind and a dash of orange liqueur (cointreau, grand marnier, etc). Sandwich the amaretti biscuits together with this and serve with coffee.

After-dinner
treats

Cointreau and cranberry fudge truffles

Makes about 50

375 g dark chocolate (1 packet Nestlé dark chocolate melts)

200 g butter

½ cup craisins (dried cranberries or substitute raisins, sultanas, etc)

¼ cup cointreau (or other orange liqueur) or freshly squeezed orange juice

grated zest of 1 orange (about 1 teaspoon)

3 cups icing sugar

750 g dark chocolate for dipping (2 packets Nestlé chocolate melts)

Melt the dark chocolate and butter together in the microwave on medium-high for about 4 minutes, stirring a couple of times during cooking. Stir in the 'craisins', liqueur or juice, orange zest and icing sugar until well combined. Chill in the fridge until firm enough to handle and roll into balls about the size of a walnut. Place the balls on a foil-lined tray and freeze until really solid, about 2 hours. Melt the 750 g of dark chocolate on medium power or over a pot of hot water. Dip the truffles in the melted chocolate. A chocolate dipping fork, which is available at good cookware shops, is invaluable for this job. Drip off excess chocolate and allow to set on a foil-covered tray. DO NOT store in the fridge as the chocolate tends to sweat, but keep them in a cool place. A good idea is to keep a plastic container of undipped truffles in the freezer, to be removed and dipped as you need them, for after-dinner treats or small gifts.

Variations

For cappuccino truffles, replace cointreau with coffee liqueur or essence and delete the craisins and grated orange rind. These can be dipped in white or dark chocolate.

Cointreau and cranberry fudge truffles

Irish cream liqueur

4 egg yolks

1 x 400 g can sweetened condensed milk

300 ml carton cream (1 small bottle or carton)

3 tablespoons chocolate dessert topping (eg. Cottees' thick and rich
   chocolate topping)

2 teaspoons coconut essence

450 ml whisky

Beat yolks until thick and pale. Add all other ingredients and beat until thick
and well combined. Store in fridge for up to 3 weeks.

Raspberry kisses

Melt 1 packet Nestlé chocolate melts (375 g) following instructions on the
packet. With a small spoon place 2 cm circles onto a tray lined with baking
paper. Place one raspberry in the centre of the circle. Remove when set.

Rum and raisin treats

Makes approximately 30

125 g butter

1 large packet marshmallows (400 g)

1 cup raisins

¼ cup rum

5–6 cups rice bubbles

1 cup melted dark chocolate

Stir butter and marshmallows over low heat until melted and well combined. Stir in raisins, rum and rice bubbles and press into a 20 × 30 cm tray lined with baking paper. Make a swirly pattern on the top with melted chocolate. Place in the fridge for 2–3 hours. When set cut into squares.

Index